The Four Boxes

Brenda Parkes
Illustrated by Oki Han

Rigby®
A Harcourt Achieve Imprint

www.Rigby.com
1-800-531-5015

Long ago an emperor
lived in a beautiful palace.

The wise old emperor had
many treasures.

But the treasures
he loved most were
his wonderful gardens
and his lovely
granddaughters.

In the soft pinks of spring,
the emperor showed
his granddaughters
the first new flowers.

Together they smelled
the scent of spring.
They flew kites
in the spring wind.

In the hot reds of summer,
he showed them colorful
butterflies and ladybugs.

Together they dipped
their toes in the pond.
They picked flowers
on warm summer nights.

In the browns and golds
of fall, he showed them
the colorful leaves
on the trees.

Together they tasted
juicy red apples.
They picked pumpkins
in the cool afternoons.

In the whiteness of winter,
he showed them trees
sparkling with ice.

Together they felt
the cold wetness of snow.
He took them skating on
the frozen pond.

One day the emperor gave
each of his granddaughters
a small wooden box.

"My body grows old," he said.
"After I die, these boxes
will help you remember the
treasures we have shared."

For many years,
the granddaughters
did not open the boxes.

When the emperor died,
the girls knew what to do.

On the first day of spring,
they went to the garden
to open the boxes.

And inside they found . . .

. . . sweet spring flowers,
warm summer sunshine,
crisp fall leaves,
and cold winter frost.

The girls knew then that
their true gifts were
the seasons they had spent
with their grandfather.

SNAKES

by
Trudi Strain Trueit

 HOUGHTON MIFFLIN   BOSTON

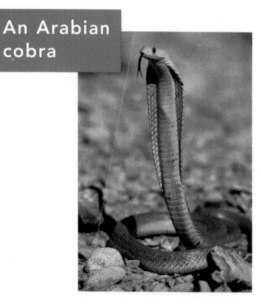

An Arabian cobra

Reading Consultant
Nanci R. Vargus, Ed.D.
Assistant Professor
Literacy Education
University of Indianapolis
Indianapolis, IN

Content Consultant
Joseph T. Collins
Director, The Center for North
American Herpetology
Lawrence, KS

Dedication:
For Austin, whose curiosity,
quest for adventure,
and laugh inspire me.

The photograph on the cover
shows a green tree viper. The
photograph on the title page
shows a blunt-headed tree snake.

Snakes by Trudi Strain Trueit. Copyright © 2003 by Children's Press. Reprinted by permission of Scholastic Inc.

Houghton Mifflin Edition

Printed in China

ISBN–13: 978-0-618-93324-2
ISBN–10: 0-618-93324-7

1 2 3 4 5 6 7 8 9 SDP 15 14 13 12 11 10 09 08

Contents

A green
tree boa

Slithering High and Low

Nearly three thousand different types of snakes live on Earth. Snakes are found on every continent in the world except Antarctica. It is too cold for snakes to live there.

Some snakes live high in the trees. Others swim deep

An olive sea snake

in the oceans. Snakes may make their homes in deserts, prairies, and maybe even your backyard.

Snakes have lived on Earth for more than 100 million

years. Snakes are reptiles.
Lizards are also reptiles.
Snakes are the most common
kind of reptile on Earth.

A Woma python in a
desert region of Australia

Snake Eyes and More

Snakes can be as thin as drinking straws or as thick as truck tires. They can be shorter than a pencil or longer than a jump rope. The Brahminy (BRAHM-ih-nee) blind snake is barely 4 inches (10 centimeters) long. The green anaconda of South America is one of the largest snakes in the world. It can be

Snakes can be as thin as the Brahminy blind snake (left) or as thick as an anaconda (below).

up to 30 feet (9 meters) long and can weigh close to 500 pounds (227 kilograms).

Every snake has a head, a body, and a tail. Long ago, snakes had legs. But over millions of years, these limbs disappeared. Pythons and boas still have tiny, claw-like remains of legs near their tails.

A snake is a vertebrate, which means it has a backbone. All snakes have at least one hundred spinal bones called vertebrae.

As this rattlesnake skeleton shows, a snake may have more than a hundred vertebrae

vertebrae

Larger snakes may have as many as four hundred vertebrae.

Snakes do not have ears on the outside of their heads. An ear bone in the jaw helps a snake pick up low sounds and vibrations.

Snakes cannot blink because they do not have movable eyelids. Clear scales called brilles cover each eye.

Have you ever seen a snake flick its tongue in and out? A snake's tongue helps it taste and smell. Each time the tongue goes out of the mouth, it picks up samples of

A snake flicks its tongue to "smell" what is nearby.

air. Each time it goes back in, it touches two holes in the roof of the snake's mouth. Inside the holes are the Jacobson's organs. These **sensory detectors** tell the snake what scents are in the air and if **predators** or **prey** are nearby.

Surprising, Scaly Skin

Snakes rely on their environments to heat their bodies. They are ectothermic (eck-tuh-THERM-ick), which means "outside heat." To get warm, a snake **basks** in the sun. To cool down, a snake rests in the shade or slips into water. Most snakes try to keep their

13

A snake warming itself in the sun

body temperature at about 86° Fahrenheit (30° Celsius). If it gets cold, a snake may **hibernate** (HI-ber-nate) until the weather turns warm again.

All snakes have scales. The scales help protect the skin. They are made of **keratin**—the same substance that makes up your fingernails.

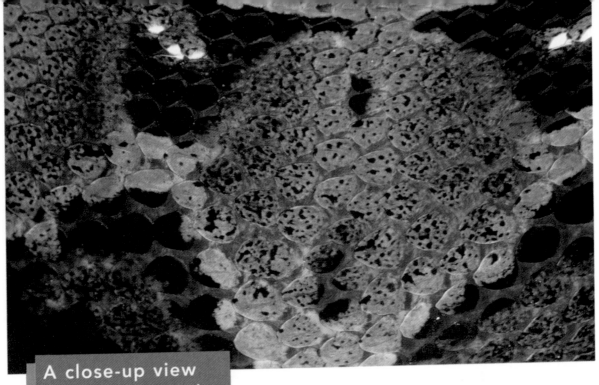

A close-up view
of a snake's scales

A snake must shed its skin
in order to grow. This is called
molting. First, a new set of
larger scales grows in under
the old ones. Then the snake
rubs its head against a rock or
the ground to peel the top

A garter snake molting

layer of skin away. The see-through skin rolls off, inside out, in one long tube. The brilles covering the snake's eyes slide off too. Adult snakes may shed their skin several times each year. Babies molt even more often.

Did You Hear Something?

A rattlesnake's buzz comes from the thick scales at the end of its tail clicking against each other. This is a warning that the snake feels threatened. Each time a rattlesnake sheds its skin, a new rattle is added. Rattlesnakes can grow up to six rattles a year. It is not true that a rattlesnake always rattles its tail before it strikes— so watch out!

A prairie rattlesnake

The Hunt

Most snakes need to eat about twice a month. Bigger snakes may eat only a few times a year. Snakes eat insects, fish, frogs, lizards, birds, rodents, eggs, small animals, and other snakes.

A snake's teeth are used only to catch and hold prey,

A snake swallowing its prey

not to chew the prey. Snakes
swallow their prey whole.

A snake can eat an animal
up to five times wider than its
own body. Special hinges in the
snake's jaws allow the snake
to open its mouth very wide.

An African egg-
eating snake
swallowing a
bird egg

The African egg-eating snake
can swallow a bird egg far
bigger than its own head. The
snake breaks the shell with its
vertebrae and later spits out
the squashed eggshell.

How can you tell that this anaconda has swallowed a large animal?

Pythons and anacondas may eat large birds, pigs, and deer. A 16-foot (5-m) African python was once found with a 130-pound (59-kg) gazelle inside it. It may take several weeks for a snake to digest such a huge meal.

A rattlesnake's fangs

Some snakes have two hollow fangs at the front or back of their mouths. When the snake bites, the fangs send liquid poison into the prey. The poison is called venom. About one-third of all snakes on Earth are venomous. Coral snakes, copperheads, cottonmouths, rattlesnakes, sea snakes, and cobras are venomous.

The king cobra is the world's largest venomous snake. It can grow to be 18 feet (5.5 m) long. Its venom is so powerful that one bite can kill an elephant. Most of the world's deadly snakes live in

A king cobra

Boas kill their prey by constriction—squeezing the prey until it can no longer breathe.

Australia, Asia, Africa, and South America. Only 15 percent of the snakes found in the United States are venomous.

Some snakes do not have fangs or venom to help them catch their prey. Instead, they coil themselves around an animal. Each time the animal takes a breath, the snake tightens its hold. Soon the prey cannot breathe. It dies from **constriction**. Boas, anacondas, and pythons are constrictors.

Zigzagging Along

Snakes travel by pushing their bodies against rocks, dirt, and grass. Many snakes, such as garter snakes and king snakes, slink along in an S-shaped path.

Larger snakes move the way a caterpillar moves—in a straight line. The long, crosswise scales on the bellies of

Garter snakes travel in an S-shaped path (top). Many large snakes, such as this yellow anaconda (bottom), move in a straight line.

boas and pythons grip the ground like the tread of a tire.

27

A tree boa looks like an accordion when it moves (top). A Mojave Desert sidewinder moves by throwing its body to the side (bottom).

Snakes that live underground or in trees look like accordions when they move. A tree boa wraps its tail around a branch, stretches forward, and pulls its tail up to wrap around a new branch farther ahead.

Desert snakes move differently than other snakes because they travel through sand that is always shifting. A desert snake lifts its head and throws its body to the side in loops. This is called sidewinding. Sidewinders can travel very quickly.

Sea snakes have tails that look like oars. Their flat tails help them glide easily through the water.

Flying snakes live in rain forests. They don't actually fly, but they come close. A flying snake leaps from a branch, flattens out its body, and glides through the air to land in another tree. The golden tree snake can "fly" more than 30 feet (9 m) in one leap.

Flying snakes can't really fly, but they can leap through the air from tree to tree.

Wriggling Babies

About three-fourths of all snakes lay eggs. The others give birth to live babies. Most snakes lay between six and thirty eggs at one time. The shells are soft and leathery. This keeps them from drying out. Once the eggs are laid, the mother leaves them. The baby snakes hatch and grow on their own.

A corn snake laying eggs (above) and corn snakes hatching (right)

It takes from six to twelve weeks for the eggs to hatch. When it is ready to be born, a baby snake uses a special tooth called an egg tooth to cut through its shell.

Some snakes, such as copperheads, give birth to live young.

Garter snakes, rattlesnakes, and boas give birth to live babies. There can be from six to one hundred babies in a single litter.

Snake eggs and young snakes are easy prey for hawks, crocodiles, wild pigs, rodents, raccoons, and other snakes.

Misunderstood Snakes

Although you may shiver when you see a snake, snakes are usually shy animals—even venomous ones. Snakes use many tricks to keep predators and people away.

Garter snakes are harmless, but may bite or release an awful odor if they're handled.

Hognose snakes, which also are
harmless, roll over and play
dead when they are afraid.

A king cobra can stretch its
body up to stand 5 feet (1.5 m)
tall. It hisses and fans out its
ribs, creating a "hood." In

Africa and Asia, spitting cobras squirt their venom as far as 7 feet (2 m) to temporarily (and sometimes permanently) blind a human or animal. This gives the snake time to escape.

A spitting cobra squirting its venom

The harmless milk snake (left) looks very similar to the venomous coral snake (right).

Coral snakes are venomous snakes that have bright red and black rings. Predators learn to avoid snakes with these markings. Some harmless snakes have similar bold

markings that fool predators. It's often hard to tell which is the venomous snake and which is not. That is why you should never touch a snake in the wild, even if you think it is not dangerous.

Hide and Seek

Can you spot the emerald tree boa? This snake's green and white markings make it look like a bunch of leaves. Snakes often use color to help them blend into their habitats. This kind of **camouflage** (CAM-uh-flawj) makes it hard for predators and prey to see them. A baby tree boa may be yellow, gold, pink, or red. As it grows, the snake changes color to match its rain-forest background.

Snakes help make sure there aren't too many rodents on Earth.

Snakes play an important role on Earth. Snakes are the main natural predators of rodents. They make sure that rats and mice do not **overpopulate** the planet. Snakes also eat animals and insects that destroy valuable food crops.

Snake venom can be "milked" from snakes and then used in medicines.

Snake venom is also useful to humans. Venom is an ingredient in many types of painkillers and medicines.

In some parts of the world, snakes are disappearing. Snakes are hunted for their skins, meat, and venom.

Sometimes snakes die because humans pollute or destroy their **habitats**. Often, snakes are killed because people are afraid of them. Perhaps the more we learn about these amazing creatures, the less we will fear them.

A Puerto Rican boa

To Find Out More

Here are some additional resources to help you learn more about snakes:

Books

Arnosky, Jim. **All About Rattlesnakes.** Scholastic Inc., 1997.

Dussling, Jennifer. **Slinky, Scaly Snakes.** Dorling Kindersley, 1998.

Martin, James. **The Spitting Cobras of Africa.** Capstone Press, 1995.

Penner, Lucille Recht. **S-S-S-Snakes.** Random House, 1994.

Pipe, Jim. **The Giant Book of Snakes and Slithery Creatures.** Copper Beech Books, 1998.

Snedden, Robert. **What is a Reptile?** Sierra Club Books for Children, 1995.

Important Words

basks warms the body by lying in the sun

camouflage the way an animal uses skin color to blend in with its surroundings

constriction being squeezed to the point where one is no longer able to breathe

habitat surroundings in which an animal lives

hibernate to go into a sleeplike state in which heart rate slows and body temperature decreases

keratin strong material that forms the scales of snakes

overpopulate to have too many of a type of animal in an environment

predators animals that hunt other animals for food

prey animals that are hunted by other animals for food

sensory detectors organs that help an animal smell, taste, see, hear, or touch

Index

46

Meet the Author

Trudi Strain Trueit is an award-winning television news reporter who has contributed stories to *ABC News*, *CBS News*, and *CNN*. Ms. Trueit has written many books for Scholastic on weather, nature, and wildlife. She is the author of three other books in the True Book series: *Lizards*, *Turtles*, and *Alligators and Crocodiles*.

Ms. Trueit loves strolling through wetlands near her home, where garter snakes can be found on the boardwalk basking in the morning sun. She lives in Everett, Washington, with her husband, Bill, a high-school teacher.

Photographs © 2003: Corbis Images/Rod Patterson/Gallo Images: 37; Dembinsky Photo Assoc.: 28 top (Claudia Adams), 27 top, 34 (E.R. Degginger), 12 (A.B. Sheldon); National Geographic Image Collection/Tim Laman: 31; Peter Arnold Inc.: 6 (Fred Bavendan), 2 (Xavier Eichaker/BIOS), 7 (J-P Ferrero/Auscape), 4 (T. Montford/BIOS), 19 (R. Andrew Odum), 42 (Roland Seitre); Photo Researchers, NY: 16 (Cosmos Blank/NAS), 41 (E. R. Degginger), 36 (Jack Dermind), 21 (Francois Gohier), 27 bottom (Claudine Laabs), 20 right, 22 (Tom McHugh), cover, 43 (John Mitchell), 17 (Rod Planck), 10 (Carl Purcell), 23 (E. Hanumantha Rao), 1 (David T. Roberts/Nature's Images Inc.), 24, 40 (Jany Sauvanet), 28 bottom, 33 top (Dan Suzio), 20 left (Karl H. Switak); Visuals Unlimited: 33 bottom (David G. Campbell), 14 (Dale Jackson), 9 right, 15, 38, 39 (Joe McDonald), 9 left (Rick Poley).